# THE SOUTHWEST: SOUTH OR WEST?

# The Southwest: *South or West?*

BY

FRANK E. VANDIVER

*Drawings by*

JO ALYS DOWNS

*Texas A&M University Press*

COLLEGE STATION

Library of Congress Cataloging in Publication Data

Vandiver, Frank Everson, 1925–
    The Southwest: South or West?

    1. Southwestern States—Civilization. I. Title.
F787.V35        979        75-16448
ISBN 0-89096-003-8

B+T

*Manufactured in the United States of America*
FIRST EDITION

To Nita, Nancy, and Bubba—
young Southwesterners

This essay represents an expansion of an address delivered to the annual meeting of the Southern Historical Association in Dallas, Texas, in November 1974.

To Nita, Nancy, and Bubba—
young Southwesterners

This essay represents an expansion of an address delivered to the annual meeting of the Southern Historical Association in Dallas, Texas, in November 1974.

# The Southwest: South or West?

SOUTHWESTERNERS tend toward slight concern for their origins, which is likely symptomatic. They assume, most of them, a certain "sportive" quality to beginnings of life in the land from the Brazos country out to the Continental Divide and down to the Great River. If the "happy accident" theory is questioned, Southwesterners might own to being Old Southern in tradition; some would say they are Western in vision. All would claim a difference peculiar to place. What are they? Will they fit a Southern mold?

Part of the answer lies in a decision on qualities of the Old South. Some lingering images of the Old South are part truth and part myth but seem the common knowledge of most people. The Old South, according to popular conception, spread across the southern reaches of the United States, was a place of mossy savannahs and slow rivers, of black men and white cotton, plantation gentlemen and hoop-skirted ladies, always a place of slowness and leisure and freedom that changed "after the war" in various ways until the South became at last James Agee's own haunt of the lost. Through the 1940's and 1950's, the South stirred in its history and was at last the ground of the Third American Revolution, the quest of blacks for justice and manhood. This revolution raged as a family quarrel about "place" for a time, then spilled out to the rest of the nation, and skirmishes were fought in such far places as Los Angeles, Detroit, and Boston. In those distant places the revolution lost its family nature to become a war of deep differences. Southerners, black and white, knew each other closely enough to compromise fairly well, and that knowledge is a key to southern history.

Now, of course, the old images are fading, ideas of "place" and race are shifting, even ideas of what the South has been. Newsmen, pundits, historians tell us so: Harry Ashmore in *Epitaph for Dixie*, Willie Morris in *North Toward Home* and *Yazoo*, even

Twelve Southerners a generation ago in *I'll Take My Stand*. Southern people have changed, made different by population shifts, by new and flourishing industry, by the United States Supreme Court, by a conscience nursed in affluence. Walter Prescott Webb, who must loom large in this discussion, once urged the South to "plow around" the racial issue, admit the burden, and get on with progress. And, in ways more spectacular than even Webb would have guessed, the South has gotten on with progress.

Images of the South hang in history, though, to charm the fancies of Americans. The images are changed now, are of a different South, one shorn of much gentility and weighted with sin. Warped images, too, clutter the Southern conscience, blurred images that refuse to mean what they seem. For history is shifting, and as the South becomes increasingly prosperous and shares the manna of the Dwindling Society, its roots are disturbed and its traditions suspect. But some verities remain: the dimly seen outline of Plato's Republic, recollections of a haven of graciousness peopled by honest folks and good, men like Thomas Jefferson, Ashley Wilkes, and General Lee. Men of this breed tended the protocols of the "country gentleman ideal," held honor dear and their

womenfolk dearer. Not women like the Scarlett O'-
Haras, but her betters, ladies as tough, but girded in
gentility. Stephen Vincent Benét catches their vel-
veted iron in *John Brown's Body.* Mary Lou Wingate
is the prototypical Southern lady:

> Her manner was gracious but hardly fervent
> And she seldom raised her voice to a servant.
> She was often mistaken, not often blind,

And she knew the whole duty of womankind,
To take the burden and have the power
And seem like the well-protected flower,
To manage a dozen industries
With a casual gesture in scraps of ease,
To hate the sin and to love the sinner
And to see that the gentlemen got their dinner
Ready and plenty and piping-hot
Whether you wanted to eat or not.
And always, always, to have the charm
That makes the gentlemen take your arm
But never the bright, unseemly spell
That makes strange gentlemen love too well,
Once you were married and settled down
With a suitable gentleman of your own.[1]

Here is a fine example of persistent mythology, true enough to survive. What the boundaries of Southern myths will be in another quarter-century is worth more speculation than space allows. Some mythological verities, too, will probably shift, some old sins may be cleansed for use, and black history

[1] Stephen Vincent Benét, *John Brown's Body* (New York: Holt, Rinehart and Winston, Inc., 1961). Copyright 1927, 1928 by Stephen Vincent Benét. Copyright renewed 1955, 1956 by Rosemary Carr Benét. Reprinted by permission of Brandt & Brandt.

may claim even the Confederacy as part of its own usable past. The South will still call beyond mere mind, will pull its people back—some kicking and screaming—with that sense of community Louis Rubin limns so well in his essay on "The Literary Community in the Old South."[2] Guilts will shift along with the "burden" of Southern history. But there will still be the old question: What is the South? And, of course, to ask the question is to acknowledge a presence.

Some novelists and romanticizers like to recall other parts of Southern mythology, the virtues of "moonlight and magnolias," the *noblesse oblige* of the planter class, and to speak wistfully of the crushed tons of crystal and shredded damask left in Sherman's wake. These lost evidences of taste stand mute indictment of Northern barbarism, a thing evident to perceptive Southerners even yet.

These traces of the popular myth have the validity of persistence, but there are other qualities of Southern history, others not so romantic: racism, bigotry, greed, those different facets of the "good, the true and the beautiful." And then, too, there is a feel

[2] In *The Writer in the South: Studies in a Literary Community* (Athens: University of Georgia Press, 1972), pp. 1–33.

for kin that runs through the Southern story, a response of blood that seems to suffuse parts of Southern life with a haunting feel of home, of place. Place is a vital touchstone to the understanding of Southerners. They *belong* somewhere, or have. Fast travel and shifting job patterns may uproot most remaining authentic Southerners. If that happens, I suspect *place* will be fulfilled by longing. "Who's your family? Where are you from?" These are still big questions in the South. Answers provide an instant rung on the social ladder. This probably will not wholly change; frames of reference are the toughest structures.

SOUTHERNERS, like all Americans, have been uncommonly restless. Their migrations westward peopled a wilderness, pushed back the Indians, and, if you like, expanded slavedom. By 1860 "the South" could be glimpsed on maps as far west as the Great American Desert. The South's vast expanse seemed large for sectional labelling, but the label ran with servitude. Was all this big country "the South?" Did the things of Southern life run beyond the Mississippi? Certainly, or, at least to some extent, obviously. Which things?

Slavery crossed the river, so the plantation system. Where these ran, so ran the South? Was there a different way of looking at life wherever these institutions were? If so, how far did they run? Where, if you will, did the West begin?

Cultural characteristics, even racial ones, do not, of course, wholly determine cultural migration. Clark Wissler thought that "topography, fauna, and flora . . . form an environment-complex, and as such go far to determine the areas of culture diffusion. . . ."[3] If Wissler is right, the West did not begin at the Missis-

[3] Clark Wissler, *Man and Culture* (New York: Crowell, 1923), quoted in Walter Prescott Webb, *The Great Plains* (Boston: Ginn and Co., 1931), p. 3.

sippi, for the "environment complex" of West Louisiana and Texas welcomed people with fauna, flora, and weather warmly similar to the Deep South. Stephen F. Austin's early Texas colonists relied on farming for sustenance and for livelihood. Cotton raising became a main interest. Labor, always a prized commodity in colonial areas, was the key to cotton's success in East Texas, and especially in the rich Brazos bottomlands. Colonists, some of them,

brought slaves, and Mexican law blinked at bondage. In the cotton regions of Texas, plantations flourished, not the manorial places of the Deep South but big, substantial spreads nonetheless that impressed—and surprised—some visitors. Surprised, because Texas seemed so far off, so rustic. And it took uncommon vision to see much social grace in that far little settlement. Houses were certainly crude by almost any standards of comparison. In Texas, clothes were rough and homespun and the niceties of culture rare and vaguely suspect. But the outlines of life were American in the Southern sense in that corner of isolation.

Cultural influence may be measured by response to progress, perhaps by response to worldly success. By this yardstick, the Brazos folk were Southerners— or wanted to be. Wealth they judged not in coin, for coin remained elusive, but in land, cotton, and slaves.

They were not really slavocrats. Eugene Genovese made a pejorative but shrewd assessment of Texas planter ideals in his observation that "even the vulgar parvenu of the Southwest embraced the plantation myth and refused to make a virtue of necessity by glorifying the competitive side of slavery as civilization's highest achievement."[4] That same Texas upstart watched each shift in Mexican attitudes toward slavery with a suspicious eye. Slavery propped the Texas economy. As American immigration grew and troubles with Mexico increased, political issues crowded the Texas consciousness, but the economy

[4] Eugene Genovese, *The Political Economy of Slavery* (New York: Vintage Books, 1967), p. 30.

and its base remained constant. In the Republic, slavery continued and grew in the cotton lands of good soil and much water.

Negro life in early Texas probably best proves the ties to the Old South. Slave conditions in Texas were somewhat easier than they were east of the Mississippi. Food was plentiful, and since most planters owned few slaves, a close relationship between master and bondsman came easily. In the Texas cotton lands black life clung to familiar protection. "Massa" gave sustenance and law, superstition and scripture gave hope, like old times before. Religion might have touched whites lightly in early Texas—Stephen Austin found "come-outerism" distasteful—but blacks listened for the promise of Canaan. Their masters, haunting for the past, might feel yesterday was better; blacks knew differently. Up yonder they would lay their burdens down.

Black allegiance to evangelical preaching worried planters in Texas, as in the eastern South. But promises of future ease had some diverting value— preachers, black and white, who called for acceptance of earthly trials were prized and encouraged. As Protestant churches grew following the Texas Revolution, many accepted black members despite their serfdom. In cotton country black preachers began to fill a spiritual need. In time there were many, and stories by and about them rang echoes of the Old South. In a remarkable book entitled *The Word on the Brazos* (Austin, 1953), J. Mason Brewer captured the rich folklore of cotton-land faith. "Preacher tales" flourished in the Carolina sea island country, the Florida east coast, and the Brazos bottoms of Texas, for the preacher was a "reckoning man."

In the big land of Texas the devil had much room for mischief. His expansive works called for heroic antidotes. Texas came to boast powerful men of the Word—folk heroes to all Texans. There was, in later days, the case of a fabled black preacher, "Sin-Killer" Griffin. As chaplain to the black convicts at the Huntsville penitentiary, Griffin found rich challenge for his talents. He had an antique art to his oratory that ran back to the oldest truths, an inborn imagery that linked him with the best of the Lord's servants. Griffin's exploits would probably, and sadly, go ridiculed today; he might lapse to the status of an Uncle Tom. But he had a lasting might of language worthy of recall. He once described the Crucifixion as he saw it:

Lightnin' played its limber gauze
When they nailed Jesus to the rugged Cross,
The mountain began to tremble
When the holy body began to drop blood
    down upon it.
Each little silver star leaped out of its orbit;
The sun went down on Calvary's bloodied brow,
Lightnin' was playin' on the horse's bridle reins
As it leaped to the battlements of glory,
When the morning star was breaking its light
On the grave.
Roman soldiers come riding in full speed
    on their horses,
And splunged Him in the side;
We seen the blood and water come out.
Oh God A'mighty placed it in the minds
    of the people
Why water is for baptism
And the blood is for cleansin'.
I don't care how mean you've been,
God A'mighty's blood'll cleanse you all from sin.[5]

For Negroes, East Texas had the travail and the
comforts of the older South. "Southwestern," people

[5] John A. Lomax, *Adventures of a Ballad Hunter* (New
York: The Macmillan Co., 1947), pp. 24, 25.

said Texas was, but that merely specified a part of the South.

For whites, too, "Southwestern" was a descriptive word, not connotative. The Republic of Texas was an American nation, distinctly of the Southern persuasion in its most populous parts. In the interior, past the wave of settlement that moved southwestward toward San Antonio, cultural imperative shifted and things were generally different.

The difference was there for anyone to see. As travelers came out of the woodlands near the middle of Texas they saw the land change. A great rumple of rock rose in a line roughly bisecting the country, a rumple formally called a "fault line": the Balcones Escarpment, which, farther north, merged into the high and awesome "caprock." Faults are geological phenomena, but the great breaking ground through Texas marked, too, a climatic difference that changed flora and fauna. The break, ranging from the 98th out beyond the 103rd meridian, seemed a kind of interior fall line. West of it level grassy prairies roamed up into brownish hills where trees grew short and scrubby, where animals shrank into tough customers who shunned water. Farther west, a semi-arid land burned under Texas sun until, at last, the Great

American Desert barred all but the hardiest animals and craziest humans. That sere ground was a frontier and likely to remain one.

That geographical frontier had a strange congruence with human frontiers. Throughout the first half of the nineteenth century waves of pioneers moved west across the American South. Those waves ebbed sometimes, even backflowed occasionally, but an inexorable taking of the open lands continued. As the American frontier advanced it wrought various kinds of newness. And there was in that process much which seemed to shape history. In 1893 Frederick Jackson Turner asserted that "American history has been in a large degree the history of the colonization of the Great West." That history reflected fascinating changes in people, Turner thought, and he offered a compelling reason. "The existence of an area of free land," he said, "its continuous recession, and the advance of American settlement westward, explain American development." "Composite nationality," democracy, and personal independence, according to Turner, had flourished because of the frontier.[6]

[6] Frederick Jackson Turner, "The Significance of the Frontier in American History," in *Proceedings of the State Historical Society of Wisconsin* (December 14, 1893).

His argument had the validity of visibility. "Westerners," a term embracing most people in the land from Texas and beyond, were clearly self-reliant folk by necessity. A man was accepted at his human value and a poignant comradeship of survival bonded the thin line of pioneers. Frontiersmen shared danger and they shared common institutions. Walter Prescott Webb, in his fascinatingly original book *The Great Plains*, caught the institutional nature of pioneering.

People coming from the eastern timberlands blundered onto the grassy plains with their thinner rivers and stunted shrubbery, and old methods of survival failed. Axes, boats, and long rifles, admirably contrived for forest life, were useless against treeless dry land and Plains Indians who warred from horseback.

Webb had one of those rare moments of insight that sometimes order the chaos of history. He was looking at the Western frontier, at the dry ground and the Plains Indians. American institutions, he saw, had to adapt in face of these challenges, and the adaptation took three salient forms: the six-shooter was adopted to subdue the Indians, barbed wire was developed to fence a treeless waste, and windmills were put to use to extract ground water for drinking and for dry farming needs. This bare recital parches Webb's thesis, but he thought in institutional terms and recognized the institutional mutations forced by the area west of the 98th meridian.

Webb's intellectual frontier expanded after he wrote *The Great Plains*; he glimpsed, in Columbus's time, a world frontier represented by the Americas, and he devoted years to a study of the boom that began in 1500 and ended only when the new hemisphere filled during the twentieth century. Always

clear-eyed and focused on challenge, Webb missed
few facets of his insights. One I think he missed, or
bypassed: the clash of two frontiers in Texas, the
cultural shock resulting when the new American
frontier met the old Spanish frontier along the edge
of southwestern settlement. Not that Webb ignores
the Spanish. In the *Great Plains*, he devotes a chapter
to "The Spanish Approach to the Great Plains," in
which he shows clearly the inadequacy of Spanish
institutional adaptation to the plains environment.
The front line of Spanish settlement thrust out in two
prongs, one toward East Texas, another toward Santa
Fe, while the center sagged to San Saba and finally
back to San Antonio.

Encomenderos, friars, and conquistadors, large plantations, missions, and presidios could not stand against nature, isolation, and fierce Indians. The Spanish colonial system failed to adapt and Spanish intrusion in the north halted. But the Spanish outposts from Santa Fe to San Antonio stabilized, and there Americans and Mexicans met. Stephen Austin's colony reflects an early attempt at cultural adjustment that failed in a welter of misunderstanding, suspicion, and racial imperatives. The cultural frontiers were mutually repelling. Texas Independence pushed Mexico's borders back, but influences remained, influences, traits, even institutions.

That area of cultural shock in the Southwest stood as real a frontier as a geographical one. Possibly Webb ignored it because it was a wholly human encounter; he was always inspired by human wars against nature. Perhaps the cultural frontier simply lacked drama for him. Whatever the reason, he remained—even after wrestling with the Great Frontier—fixed toward the geographical west. In a marvelously interpretive essay titled "What is 'the West'?" published in 1957, Webb inadvertently explained his blind spot when defining one he saw in Westerners. "Those who live in it or around its

borders, as all Westerners do, should not avoid facing
the Desert, whose near presence gives them their chief
problems, makes them Westerners."[7] He avoided
looking South, he turned from cultural clash and saw
land as the place of challenge.

Webb offers a definition that, if accepted, answers the question posed earlier: "Where does the
West begin?" For him, for most students in his wake,
the West begins at that interior fall line where water
runs scarce. Those Americans with Southern back-
grounds who crossed the Mississippi would agree
with that geographical boundary. Beyond that barrier

[7] Webb's essay is in Robert W. Howard, ed., *This Is the
West* (New York: New American Library, 1957), pp. 16–17.

precious little grew; the plantation idea would not work. The notion of a natural limit to plantation-slave expansion terrified many pre-war Southern politicians and consoled some abolitionists. Daniel Webster had no worries about admitting western states to the Union; the desert would keep free. By 1861 his guess proved out. Although the Confederacy cherished hopes of including New Mexico and Arizona, these regions were by nature foreign soil. Expeditions to the arid lands failed as much from lack of conviction as from military defeat. The Cotton Kingdom stopped where water stopped.

Past central Texas, life looked too hard for the effort. Hardy Indians survived by nomadic search for waterholes, buffalo, and elusive desert game. Some straggling settlements lingered at Santa Fe, in scattered New Mexico and Arizona patches, settlements founded on trade routes and marginal food production. People out there were present-minded. Daily challenge denied such formal realities as lineage, tradition, or high education. If the Confederacy represented a crusade for the past, it had no chance to win the West.

Did it have a chance in the area widely accepted as the Southwest—in the Indian country spanning the Red River, in South Central Texas, and on to the Mexican border? Apparently yes, by all indications. This section, with its settlements spreading north to New Braunfels and west to other German towns, had long been a scene of triangular trouble between whites, Mexicans, and Indians. But Mexican life patterns were closer to Southern than Western; the encomienda could, with loose construction, be called a plantation. Filibusters of earlier days had talked of a great slavocracy that would encompass a golden circle including Mexico and Cuba. Slavery existed in Hispaniola and peonage continued in Mexico. As things worked out, Mexico halfheartedly flirted with the Confederacy for political, not cultural, reasons, and no alliance formed. Race still kept its frontiers.

More importantly, though, the Confederacy had trouble holding on to the Americanized area in the western South. The vast Trans-Mississippi Department—West Louisiana, Arkansas, Texas, and the Treaty Indian nations—felt aloof from Richmond's concerns, at length even alienated from an extractive war effort. In that domain, colloquially called Kirby-Smithdom after the Confederate commanding general Edmund Kirby Smith, natural independence bloomed. Out there, remote from most of the war, meanings changed and words were different. Victory became survival. True, thousands of Rebel troops went from the Trans-Mississippi to eastern theaters, much treasure went to Confederate coffers, thousands of civilians sacrificed for political independence. But distance dimmed enchantment and enthusiasm waned without crisis. The West had too much future to struggle for the past. Finally Kirby-Smithdom virtually sloughed the war and turned from the failed Old South.

War worked vast changes in Southern life. Defeat separated the ex-Rebel states even farther from the American way. Slavery went, the plantation system shifted scope and size, poverty passed for gentility; military occupation shattered the image of freedom. For the Old South the past clearly was better than the future.

In the former Trans-Mississippi Department the future looked bleak enough, especially in the cotton reach along the Brazos. But postwar depression brought only fleeting despair.

Why? Possibly because life had always been uncertain in the Southwest. Depression seemed nat-

ural. And in a frontier world, people thought they might have a handle on tomorrow. After all, life had been a lot tougher in Republic days. Energy and gumption had always improved things; no reason to doubt them now. Texas had long been a land of hope and escape, as attested by hundreds of doors back east daubed with the boast "Gone to Texas!" Progress had been steady in the Southwest and would continue, once adjustments to Northern peace were made.

T HE biggest adjustment would be to find a substitute for cotton, a substitute in economic demand

and one that could be produced without slave labor. By the end of the 1860's the range cattle industry showed promise of being the substitute. And with railroads inching out on the plains to Sedalia, Missouri, and Abilene, Kansas, great cattle drives could reach markets. A new era in use of the prairie plains began. Cattle dethroned cotton in the western kingdom and great herds built great fortunes—sometimes.

Webb recognized the range cattle business as a response to challenges both physical and economic and saw the drives as possible only in a vast free domain without forests and fences. And the cattle business did provide capital in the post-war depression. But it did more than that. It provided a new mythology, one that built on earlier myths to form, at last, one of America's greatest escape routes from reality.

Considerable mythology gathered around the West from earliest American migration. Foreign travelers, and these included eastern Americans, were fascinated by the newness, the sprawling openness, and the possibilities of the land. Indians always drew wide-eyed wonder and sparked fantastic tales of deeds to rival Mike Fink's triumphs. But the full-blown myths of a wild and carefree life began with the day of the cowboy. Daring, strong, courtly, the

western cowboy worked hard, played harder, and lived a life largely devised by the likes of Ned Buntline and Zane Grey. Probably more boys were lured from the huddled East by dime-novel cowboys than by the naughty charms of the circus!

Myths that persist serve a deep human need. The cowboy myth filled many needs. A cowboy's freedom fascinated city-bound youths; his bravery and chivalry fitted girls' hopes for real men. He was whang-leather tough and good with a gun, and men wanted to be like him. Books and articles galore told the cowboy's tale. Here and there some carping voice would squawk in envious opposition. A few bookish folk argued that the cowboy's life was squalid, that he was mortal, even mean. But good myths work their own truth and people know what to believe. So the cowboy legend grew as did that of his Indian foemen, reached back across the East, skipped oceans, and became well-nigh universal. The American West became a "state of mind," a Camelot for millions.

The cowboy myth persists, of course, now personified by John Wayne, who triumphs nightly on myriad television screens. According to the present legend, the cowboy has much of the Southerner in him—Owen Wister and Randolph Scott wrote and fleshed the script—for he hews hard to the cavalier ideal. Much of cowboy mythology comes from a special branch of folklore, a branch John Lomax made peculiarly his own—cowboy songs. Singing served as a handy time-passer on the range and sometimes soothed restless cattle. Lomax, who collected Western ballads in a long career of interviewing and listening, heard the history of an era. He noted in his quest for the old, authentic music, that it changed with time and place, but that moods usually stayed constant. Cowboys told their woes to music, bragged their fun, their hopes, and triumphs in songs good, bad, and awful. Western songs hinted at Southern ancestry; many were versions of folksongs harking back to Old

England. They evolved in the West from roisterous autobiographies into laments for a better life. And they became increasingly salable as "old-time" music, then as "hillbilly," and now as "country western" and "progressive country."

Life and movement filled the earlier songs:

Come along, boys, and listen to my tale;
　"I'll tell you of my troubles on the
　　Old Chisholm Trail . . . .
With a ten dollar hoss and a forty-dollar saddle

I'm goin' to punchin' Texas cattle....
Stray in the herd, and the boss said kill it,
So I buried that stray in the bottom
of a skillet....

Some told the whole of cowboy history:

I rode a line on the open range
When cowpunching wasn't slow;
I've turned the longhorned cow one way,
And the other the buffalo....
I've been in many a stampede, too;
I've heard the rumbling noise;
And the light we had to turn them by
Was the lightning on their horns....
The old cowboy has watched the change,
Has seen the good times come and go;
But the old cowboy will soon be gone
Just like the buffalo.[8]

There was, too often, bitter acceptance of a hard fate

[8] R. E. Lingenfelter, R. A. Dwyer, and David Cohen, comps. and eds., *Songs of the American West* (Berkeley and Los Angeles: University of California Press, 1968), p. 409. Originally published by the University of California Press; reprinted by permission of The Regents of the University of California.

reflected in the cowboy's music. Surely the best example is "The Dying Cowboy":

> Oh, bury me not on the lone prairie,
>> In a little grave just six by three,
> Where the coyotes howl and the wind blows free.

Nostalgia lends a rosy hue to "country westerns" now. Many current songs are full of remembrance of freer days and that old-time selfless romance. Consider, for example, "Don't Fence Me In," and Marty Robbins's hit, "El Paso." In these new "authentic" songs—not the "rock-a-billy" sound—mythic virtues and principles still prevail. There is a touching recognition of a present need for the unreal West.

Cut down to realities, the cowboy lived a lonesome, grubby life, starved and ate dust on the trail, brawled in booming cowtowns, and took women as they were. But he did have freedom, nourished the special comradeship of the plains, and knew men when he met them. He was something like the ultimate frontiersman. Old Southerner he was not. Though he might long for home and family, he roamed a world without roots and earned status by manhood. He did not prevail beyond the boundaries of the cattle kingdom and he rarely rode the desert.

His true trail ran south across the Rio Grande to encomienda country. In Mexico, where the hacienda sometimes shamed the plantation house, his roots could be found. The cowboy was a Southwestern phenomenon. His day lasted as long as free land lasted. His legend, I suggest, will last as long as people want to be brave and free and real.

That legend, full panoplied with six guns, bad-men, and wild stampedes, lingers as one of the few traditions of the Southwest—a region that had to grow its own. Nationalism is probably another South-western tradition, nationalism taking local form and expressed in prideful bragging. Southwesterners de-veloped an almost Southern fierceness about their do-main. Texans boasted loudest, firm on the Republic's base, disdainful of the dry-ground folk of New Mexi-co, Arizona, and the Oklahoma territory. Pride of place shows often in seriocomic rivalries and stories. Oklahomans, long sufferers of Texas boasting, de-veloped a defensive folklore. One story will suffice. In early days of Oklahoma settlement, pioneers trekked south and came one day to a sign: "Texas Begins Here." Those who could read, stopped.

This fierce patriotism also cherishes the short and local history of plains settlement. Old history is re-spected, not loved. Generations of schoolchildren know Southwestern lore as original scripture. They know, too, that local heroes are epic figures and that most of these are, please pardon the expression, Texans.

Austin, Sam Houston, Ben McCulloch, Charles Goodnight, L. H. McNelly of the Texas Rangers, all were tough customers, equal to the Santa Annas, Sam Basses, and John Wesley Hardins. But nonetheless they were lesser mortals, for they were measured against the Alamo's defenders. Romantics, having bowed toward the Alamo, usually turn to the Bat Mastersons and Wyatt Earps as prodigal lawmen, to Billy the Kid and the Clanton gang as heroic villains. Western heroes are mainly fighters and among the best of these, naturally, must number Cochise, Mangas Coloradas, Satanta, and Satank.

There is a striking similarity between Indian and Southwestern American heroes. Warrior virtues they shared, hardihood, persistence, even violence, and the grudging admiration of old enemies. Texas and Arizona rangers knew Indian ways and wiles, understood Indians far better than eastern or southern neighbors. Was this the kinship of animosity showing, or was it because both were frontiersmen? Whatever the cause, the result is a striking cultural sharing.

White Southwesterners were more borrowers than sharers. From "home," mainly the South back East, they borrowed less than expected, but some things lasted. Religion, for example, followed the

frontier and was at least somewhat changed by it. Catholicism enjoyed established favors in colonial days but never caught on much with Texans, although the Mexican population kept the faith. Frontier life offered varied rivals for Sunday time and the foreign formalism of a Latin service resisted enthusiasm. Enthusiasm seemed essential in a preacher after the Civil War. Morals slipped in post-war society and cowboys had considerable affinity for Bacchus. As it had been on older frontiers, so in the Southwest. Evangelical congregations flourished and in time the Baptists gained dominance, with Methodists running second. One observer opined that Baptists ran Texas, "but the Methodists own the place."[9] Baptists stood against

[9] Quoted in Donald Day, *Big Country: Texas* (New York: Duell, Sloan and Pearce, 1947), p. 294.

most cowboy ways, apparently against most kinds of fun. But their stern morality spread, largely because of talented exhorters who knew how to get attention. In the outlaw days, when gunmen were plentiful and sin gaining, an ex-gambler and bartender turned parson, Andrew Jackson Potter, found himself in a small West Texas town on Sunday. He found no church, no proper preaching place, so he commandeered the saloon. Outside he stationed an "announcer" primed to draw an audience in proper Southwestern parlance:

> Oyez, oyez, there's goin' to be some hellfired racket here this mornin', gents, by Fightin' Parson Potter, a reformed gambler, gents, but now a shore-nuff gospel shark. It's a-goin' to begin in fifteen minutes, gents; all ye old whiskey soaks an' card sharks better come on over an' learn to mend yer ways or the devil's gonna get ye quicker'n hell can scorch a feather.[10]

Whether by God's grace or in spite of it, prosperity came to the area—in spots. And people took on trappings of society as they could. Cities grew and built churches and installed loud criers of the Word. Of all cultural imperatives, religion seemed to tie the

[10] Ibid., p. 296.

Southwest closest to the Old South, religion both black and white. To the blacks, faith still gave hope even in the hard Ku Klux Klan years and the time of iron segregation. Religion provided whites various justifications.

$A$ s the nineteenth century dwindled and the United States enjoyed the Gilded Age and Populism, Southwesterners shared the plaints of farmers everywhere. Farming came strongly to Texas and its neighbors after the Civil War, small farming until the good grain and cotton lands of the Panhandle Plains introduced commercial agriculture in the twentieth century. Small farmers tended toward a mild radicalism save in the South, where the shackles of defeat clapped an iron conservatism on most minds and spirits. In Texas and the Southwest, radicalism took a stronger form. Agricultural protest societies flourished, even to the extent of trying biracial organization.[11]

According to the director of the census in 1890, the American frontier no longer existed. That star-

[11] William F. Holmes, "The Demise of the Colored Farmers' Alliances," *The Journal of Southern History* 41 (May 1975): 187–200.

tling assertion fell largely unnoticed on an indifferent society. But students of frontier effects later would see that a whole American epoch ended. If the frontier had indeed shaped much of America's character, what would its passing mean? Virtually nothing to a nation about to realize its manifest destiny around the globe. For the Southwest, though, the passing of the frontier meant that the openness would likely close, that the great cattle ranges would spawn fences and such other excrescences as sheep and sodbusters. Cattle might not be king for long.

That turned out to be true, but by the time it happened, cotton and cattle were already challenged by a slick intruder on the Southwestern scene—oil. After the big oil discovery at Spindletop in 1901 came natural gas and the burgeoning business of refining and distribution. So glittering were oil's prospects that it spawned a new type of frontiersman, the wildcatter. In his own way he lived the life of a latter-day cowboy—nomadic, gambling with the future, often down but rarely out.

Big strikes and new fields ushered in the huge corporate stage of oil development and oil shoved cotton and cattle aside as the Southwest's major wealth producer. First strikes were followed by brief

recessions in the industry as drilling and refining techniques lagged. World War I demands encouraged new discoveries, however, and by the mid-1920's overproduction loomed an ominous threat to the world oil market. Restrictions slowed but could not stop increasing reserves.

Depression helped cool demands for oil, and the business did not recover until World War II launched the Age of Gasoline. Depression, too, hit hard at cattle raisers in the Southwest. Cotton and wheat growers suffered price collapse and endured slow, painful recovery. The entire area shared the doldrums of the 1930's.

After World War II petroleum and petro-chemicals ignited a Southwestern boom that the recent energy crisis has only increased. Entrepreneurs replaced most of the wildcatters, but oilmen are still, most of them, a frontier breed.

Cotton, cattle, and oil are the tools of Southwestern progress. But men found the tools and had the vision to use them. In the growing cities of the Southwest there is yet a feeling of the frontier, a sense of things unfinished, of chances to be taken. Southwesterners now boast considerable sophistication, parade it at symphony performances, theaters, universities, in jet-setter salons everywhere. But they are happiest in contests, in business conflicts, in politics— and that may explain the regional hysteria for football.

Heroes remain much the same, people to compete and prevail. The Austins and Houstons, Ashbel Smiths and Will Hoggs yielded to the Jesse Joneses, Will Claytons, the Tom Slicks, Harry Sinclairs, "Dad" Joiners, Walter Webbs, Will Rogerses, then to the Oveta Hobbys, George Browns, the Barry

Goldwaters, Barbara Jordans, and Lyndon Johnsons. Johnson is a special case, a kind of New Deal Populist with roots deep in the Southwest who held to an old Southern sense of the fitness of things and became a leading warrior in the battle for civil rights. Johnson and the others share with their fellow Southwesterners a zest for being, an excitement of vision, and conviction of good times coming.

Look at Southwesterners closely and traces of the South can be glimpsed clearly: a sense of honor, a code of courtesy, a feeling for place, a belief that people are more important than things or ideas. An evil Southern trace, too, can sometimes be seen: a strong racial feeling that has hindered and confused life in the Southwest, tarnished its glitter and dimmed its promise. But the racial imperative is, as Webb hoped, weakening against a Western willingness to take men for themselves in a common race for the future. Traces of Spain show, too, in Southwesterners: a generous spirit, an easy hospitality, appreciation of living, a graceful, indigenous architecture, and picante cooking. A certain canny toughness comes surely from the Plains Indians.

Are modern Southwesterners the sum of these traces? Yes, but with an extra ingredient to make them uniquely Southwestern. They cannot be wholly understood apart from the land that nurtures them, that land from the Red River, west to the Sierras and south to the Rio Grande, a land of varied plenty, unhampered by too much harsh history, a place still becoming something. Southwesterners see the future as a frontier; they are essentially tomorrow's folk.